A Guide
to
APA
Documentation

A Guide
to
APA
Documentation

Joseph F. Trimmer

Ball State University

Australia • Brazil • Japan • Korea • Mexico • Singapore • Spain • United Kingdom • United States

A Guide to APA Documentation
Joseph F. Trimmer

Senior Publisher: Lyn Uhl

Acquisitions Editor: Kate Derrick

Development Editor: Kathy Sands-Boehmer

Assistant Editor: Cat Salerno

Editorial Assistant: Abbie Rickard

Media Editor: Cara Douglass-Graff

Marketing Manager: Stacey Purviance

Marketing Communications Manager:
Courtney Morris

Marketing Coordinator: Brittany Blais

Content Project Manager: Aimee
Chevrette Bear

Art Director: Jill Ort

Print Buyer: Betsy Donaghey

Rights Acquisition Specialist: Amber Hosea

Production Service: MPS Limited,
A Macmillan Company

Compositor: MPS Limited, A Macmillan
Company

© 2013 Wadsworth, Cengage Learning

For product information and technology assistance, contact us at
Cengage Learning Customer & Sales Support, 1-800-354-9706

For permission to use material from this text or product,
submit all requests online at **www.cengage.com/permissions**.
Further permissions questions can be emailed to
permissionrequest@cengage.com.

Library of Congress Control Number: 2011933051

ISBN-13: 978-0-840-03010-8

ISBN-10: 0-840-03010-X

Wadsworth
20 Channel Center Street
Boston, MA 02210
USA

Cengage Learning is a leading provider of customized learning solutions with office locations around the globe, including Singapore, the United Kingdom, Australia, Mexico, Brazil, and Japan. Locate your local office at:
international.cengage.com/region

Cengage Learning products are represented in Canada by Nelson Education, Ltd.

For your course and learning solutions, visit **www.cengage.com**.

Purchase any of our products at your local college store or at our preferred online store **www.cengagebrain.com**.

Instructors: Please visit **login.cengage.com** and log in to access instructor-specific resources.

Printed in the United States of America
2 3 4 5 6 7 15 14

Contents

This booklet explains the documentation style recommended by the American Psychological Association (APA) for citing references in research papers commonly written in the social sciences. It analyzes some of the implications of using APA style in your research and composing. It also offers examples of how to use in-text citations and footnotes, how to prepare the list of references, and how to organize the format of an APA research paper, and it provides an annotated student research paper. More detailed information on these procedures can be found in the *Publication Manual of the American Psychological Association.*[1]

1. Research and Composition

APA style emphasizes the importance of following the procedures for planning and writing the research paper outlined in any standard writing textbook. In particular, APA style asks you to devote considerable attention to certain steps in your research and composing.

Evaluating References

As you begin collecting references to advance your research, evaluate them according to the following criteria:

1. **A reference should be relevant.** Ask yourself, "Does the content in this reference apply directly to the topic of my paper?" Whether a particular reference is relevant is not always directly apparent. When you begin your research, your lack of perspective on your subject may make every reference seem potentially relevant. Titles of references may also be misleading or vague, prompting you to examine a reference that has no relationship to your subject, or to dismiss a reference that seems too theoretical or general when it actually could give you vital perspectives on your subject. The status of your

---

[1]American Psychological Association. (2009). *Publication manual of the American Psychological Association* (6th ed.). Washington, DC: Author.

references may also change as you restrict or redefine your subject. A reference that seemed irrelevant yesterday may appear more essential today. For example, you may come across a reference on garbage in your search for information on alternate forms of energy that seems irrelevant. But as you narrow your research to focus on how certain substances can be used for fuel, the source that discusses garbage may seem suddenly relevant.

2. **A reference should be authoritative.** Ask yourself, "Does the author of a particular reference have the necessary expertise or experience to speak authoritatively about the subject of my paper?" Most print sources enable you to judge the credentials and biases of the author. You can usually judge the authority of an article or book because it has been reviewed by knowledgeable peers—experts on the subject under consideration. But you may have no way to evaluate the authority of many electronic sources. A source you assume is authoritative may have been posted by a hacker or someone who wishes to further his or her own agenda. For example, some Wikipedia entries are submitted by people who have no real expertise on a subject but want to distort it or spin it in a slanted direction.

3. **A reference should be current.** Ask yourself, "Is this source current?" You don't want to cite a 50-year-old reference if you are writing about the latest cures for cancer. However, you may want to use that 50-year-old reference if you are writing about the history of cancer therapy. Writers often cite standard print references to establish the reliability of their arguments. Then they will cite recent electronic references to address issues that have arisen since the print references were originally published. Keep in mind that electronic references are not necessarily the most current, since many print references are now posted online. To make sure your references are reliable and current, you may need to mix print and electronic sources.

4. **A reference should be comprehensive.** Ask yourself, "Does this reference cover all the major issues I want to discuss in my paper?" Some sources will focus on an extremely narrow aspect of your subject; others will cover every feature and many related, or unrelated, topics as well. Begin reading the most comprehensive first because it will cover all the essential information in the more specialized references and provide information on many related subtopics within your subject. Most books, for example, are comprehensive references, whereas many online sites provide only "bits" of information.

5. **A reference should be stable.** Ask yourself, "If I use this reference, will my readers be able to locate it if they want to read more about the topic of my paper?" You want to cite references that provide the best and most stable information on your topic. There is nothing more stable than a book. Even if you library does not own a book or if the book is out of print, librarians can find a copy for your readers through interlibrary loan. The same is true for most articles. But electronic

references are not always stable. The reference you stumble on today may not be there tomorrow. Your readers will not be able to find it because it may have been renamed, reclassified, or simply deleted. If your readers want to check your references, you should cite references they can find. Again, Wikipedia is not a stable source because entries are often added and deleted so often that your readers may not be able to find the source you want to quote.

6. **A reference should provide links.** Ask yourself, "Does this reference help me locate other references?" The best references lead to other references, which can further your research. The subject headings on a reference provide an excellent system for linking up with other references. Annotated bibliographies at the back of some references not only link you to other references but also provide you with an assessment of their value. Of course, the chief advantage of the web and its various search engines is that they allow you to link up with thousands of references by simply pointing and clicking. If your reference provides such links, your readers can use them to trace the research that informs the reference and the way you have used it to broaden and deepen the research in your paper.

Recording Reference Information

Once you have located references you believe will prove useful, fill out a source card or create a computer file for each item. List the references in the appropriate format. (Use the formats shown in the guidelines for "Preparing List of References," pages 10–22.) To guarantee that each card or file is complete and accurate, take your information about print references directly from the source rather than from the online catalogue or bibliographic index. However, because online references have such long and complicated search data, you should print out the reference as it is displayed on your screen. Your collection of cards or files will help you track your references throughout your research. Alphabetizing the cards or files will enable you to prepare a provisional list of references.

This provisional list must be in place *before* you begin writing your paper. You may expand or refine the list as you write, but to provide an appropriate in-text citation as you write, you first need to know the correct citation for your reference. Thus, although the list of references will be the last section of your paper, you will need to prepare a preliminary version of it first.

Taking Notes

Note taking demands that you read, select, interpret, and evaluate the information that you plan to cite in your paper. After you have returned material to the library or turned off your computer, your notes will be the only record of your research. If you have taken notes carelessly, you will be in trouble when you use them in your paper. Many students inadvertently plagiarize because they work from inaccurate note cards. (See "Avoiding Plagiarism," pages 6–8.)

If you are relying on your computer to create reference files, you may also commit plagiarism by falling into the "copy-paste trap." The most efficient way to work with electronic sources is to copy important passages from online sources and the paste them into your research files. But this quick and easy way of saving information can also get you into a lot of trouble. If you simply "save" the material you have found without marking it as a quotation and identifying its source, you may assume that you composed the sentences you see pasted in your file and present them as your own writing.

As you select information from a reference, use one of three methods to report it: quoting, summarizing, or paraphrasing.

Quoting References

Although quoting an author's text word for word is the easiest way to report information, you should use this method selectively and quote only passages that deal directly with your subject in memorable language. When you copy a quotation onto a note card or paste it into a file, place quotation marks at the beginning and end of the passage. If you decide to omit part of the passage, use ellipsis points to indicate that you have omitted words from the original source. To indicate the omission from the middle of the sentence, use three periods (. . .) and leave a space before and after each period. To indicate the omission of the end of the sentence or more than one sentence, use three spaced periods following the sentence period (. . . .).

To move the quotation from your notes into your paper, making it fit smoothly into the flow of your text, use one of the following methods:

1. **Work the quoted passage into the syntax of your sentence.**

   Igo (2007) pointed out that those who have analyzed the research methods of the social sciences have focused on those who have conducted the studies rather than on "what ordinary people, 'the studied,' did with the . . . information" (p. 13).

2. **Introduce the quoted passage with a complete sentence and a colon.**

   Commentators who have studied the findings of social science research have focused too much on the producers of new knowledge: "Few have paid attention to what ordinary people, 'the studied,' did with the . . . information" (Igo, 2007, p. 13).

3. **Set off the quoted passage with an introductory phrase or sentence followed by a colon.**

   This method is reserved for passages of 40 or more words. Double-space the quotation, and indent it 1 inch (10 spaces) from the left margin.

Because this special placement identifies the passage as a quotation, *do not* enclose it within quotation marks. Notice that the final period goes *before* rather than *after* the parenthetical reference. Leave one space after the final period.

Igo (2007) found the following:

> Even those attentive to the uses of social scientific authority have generally asked how elites—whether states, corporations, or courts—mobilized empirical data for particular ends. Few have paid attention to what ordinary people, "the studied," did with the . . . information. (p. 13)

Summarizing and Paraphrasing References

Summarizing and paraphrasing an author's text are the most efficient ways to report information. The terms *summary* and *paraphrase* are often used interchangeably to describe a brief restatement of the author's ideas in your own words, but they may be used more precisely to designate different procedures. A *summary* condenses the argument of a source. When you write a summary, you reformulate the main point of the author's argument. A *paraphrase* restates the content of a short passage. When you paraphrase, you reconstruct the passage phrase by phrase, recasting the author's words in your own words.

A summary or paraphrase is intended as a complete and objective presentation of the author's ideas, so be careful not to distort the original argument by adding your own opinion or slanting the original passage by omitting major points. Because the words of a summary or paraphrase are yours, they are not enclosed by quotation marks. But because the ideas you are restating came from someone else, you need to cite the source in your notes and in your text. (See "Avoiding Plagiarism," pp. 6–8.)

The following examples illustrate two common methods for introducing a summary or a paraphrase into your paper:

1. **Summary of an author's major argument.** *(See the Igo quotation above.)*

   Often the best way to proceed is to name the author of the source (and its date) at the beginning of your sentence. This procedure informs your reader that you are about to summarize someone else's research. It also gives you an opportunity to state the credentials of the authority you are citing.

   > Prominent social scientist Igo (2007) has discovered that authorities have seemed to focus on the evidence compiled by studies—opinion polls, surveys, community studies, and consumer research—rather than on how such evidence has become part of everyday life.

2. **Paraphrase of a short quotation.** *(See second sentence of the Igo quotation on page 5.)*

You may decide to vary the pattern of your in-text citation if you are presenting a paraphrase of a specific passage by including the author's name, date of publication, and page number in parentheses at the end of your sentence. This method is particularly useful if you have already established the identity of your source in a previous sentence and now want to focus on the author's ideas in some detail without having to clutter your sentences with constant references to his or her name.

> Authorities have often focused on the evidence compiled by social science researchers instead of analyzing how the people who were the subject of such studies were affected by them (Igo, 2007, p. 13).

References

Igo, S. E. (2007). *The averaged American: Surveys, citizens, and making of mass*

   public. Cambridge, MA: Harvard University Press.

Avoiding Plagiarism

Plagiarism is theft. It is using someone else's words or ideas without giving proper credit—or without giving any credit at all—to the author(s) of the original work. Whether plagiarism is intentional or unintentional, it is a serious offense that your instructor and school will deal with severely. You can avoid plagiarism by adhering scrupulously to the following advice:

1. **Document your references whenever you.**

   - use a direct quotation;
   - summarize or paraphrase an argument or passage in your own words;
   - copy a table, chart, or other diagram;
   - construct a table from data provided by others; and
   - present specific examples, figures, or factual information that you have taken from a specific source and used them to explain or support your argument.

2. **Take notes carefully,** making sure that you identify quotations in your note cards or electronic files. Also, be sure to identify the passage in your notes that you have recorded as a summary or paraphrase. (See "Taking Notes," page 4.)

3. **Analyze the differences between the following examples.**

   The following excerpt (Original Passage) is from Christopher Vye, Kathlene Scholljegerdes, and I. David Welch's *Under Pressure and Overwhelmed: Coping with Anxiety in College.* The first two examples (Versions A and B) illustrate how students committed plagiarism by trying to use the source in their text. The last example (Version C) illustrates how a student avoided plagiarism by carefully citing and documenting the reference.

Original Passage

Many anxiety symptoms and problems can be overcome. In fact, anxiety may be the most treatable of all mental health difficulties. Whether or not your experience of anxiety constitutes a mental health problem, decades of research have provided a wealth of valuable information.*

Version A

Many anxiety symptoms and problems can be overcome. Anxiety may be the most treatable of all mental health difficulties. Whether your experience of anxiety constitutes a mental health difficulty, decades of research have provided a wealth of valuable information.

Version A is plagiarism. Because the writer of Version A does not indicate in the text or in a parenthetical reference that the words and ideas belong to Vye, Scholljegerdes, and Welch, her readers will believe the words are hers. She has stolen the words and ideas and has attempted to cover the theft by changing or omitting an occasional word.

Version B

Many anxiety symptoms and problems can be overcome. In fact, anxiety may be the most reatable of all mental health difficulties. Whether or not your experience of anxiety constitutes a mental health problem, decades of research have provided a wealth of valuable information (Vye, Scholljegerdes, & Welch, 2007).

Version B is also plagiarism, even though the writer acknowledges his reference in an in-text citation. He has worked from careless notes and misunderstood the difference between quoting and paraphrasing. He has copied the original passage word for word yet supplied no quotation marks to indicate the extent of his borrowing. As written and documented, the passage masquerades as a paraphrase when in fact it is a direct quotation.

*Vye I., Scholljegerdes, K. & Welch, I. D. (2007). *Under pressure and overwhelmed: Coping with anxiety in college.* Westport, CT: Praeger.

Version C

Vye, Scholljegerdes, and Welch (2007) have indicated that while anxiety may be a common problem, it "may be the most treatable of all mental health difficulties . . . [and that] decades of research have provided a wealth of valuable information" (p. 9).

Version C is one satisfactory way of handling this source material. The writer has identified the authors of her reference at the beginning of her sentence, letting her readers know who is about to be quoted. She then introduces the concept of anxiety in her own words, placing quotation marks around the parts of the original passage she wants to quote, using ellipsis points to delete the parts of the passage she wants to omit, and inserting brackets to enable her to add words to create a coherent sentence. In an in-text citation she provides a reference to the page number in the source listed in the references.

References

Vye I., Scholljegerdes, K., & Welch, I. D. (2007). *Under pressure and*

overwhelmed: Coping with anxiety in college. Westport, CT: Praeger.

2. Documenting References

To avoid clutter in your sentences, APA recommends that when you cite a reference for the first time, use the author(s)' last name(s) and date of publication at the beginning of your sentence. Notice in the example here that the authors' names appear in the order presented on the title page (*not* alphabetically) and are separated by an *and*. When you cite authors' names in an in-text citation or in the list of references, you should use an ampersand (&) rather than an *and*. Also notice that the sentence is written in the past tense to indicate that the authors published their conclusions at a specific time in the past (2007). Because the writer is summarizing the authors' general argument, specific page numbers are not included. (See "Summarizing and Paraphrasing," pp. 5–6.)

Engell and Dangerfield (2007) concluded that the crisis in higher education has been caused by the obsession with market values.

When you cite a reference a second time, you may decide to place the authors' last names and date of publication in parentheses at the end of the sentence but before the final period. Notice in the next example that the writer includes a specific page number to indicate that she is paraphrasing a specific passage.

A recent study determined that the ends of higher education are dedicated to making money rather than teaching critical thinking and cultural values (Engell & Dangerfield, 2007, p. 2).

When you include a long quotation in your text, as in the following example, place the relevant information for the in-text citation at the end of the passage but *after* the final period. (See "Quoting References," pp. 4–9.)

Engell and Dangerfield (2007) argued that the crisis in higher education was caused by a preoccupation with money:

> Money, rather than means, is becoming the chief end of higher education. The rationale to pursue and practice higher education is now routinely predicated not on learning but on money. With growing frequency, the ends are not cultural values or critical thinking, ethical convictions or intellectual skills. When those goals are pursued, it is often not because they offer multiple uses and relevance but because they might be converted into cash. (p. 2)*

References

Engell, J., & Dangerfield, A. (2007). *Saving higher education in the age of money*.

Charlottesville, VA: University of Virginia Press.

3. Using Footnotes

In APA style, footnotes allow you to provide additional commentary and clarification on the information in your text that, although important, might disrupt the flow of your paper. APA recommends that such footnotes be included only if they strengthen your argument. APA also recommends that such footnotes convey just one idea each.

In the text of your paper, designate a footnote by placing a superscript number at the end of your sentence, like this.[1] Then at the "foot" or bottom of the page, use the same superscript number to mark the content of the note you wish to add. All such footnotes should be numbered sequentially throughout your paper.

An alternative method for listing notes is to create a separate note page, titled "Notes," on which you can arrange your notes in the numerical sequence in which they appear in your text. This page should be placed *after* the References page.

> Thurber's reputation continued to grow until the 1950s, when he was forced to give up drawing because of his blindness.[1]

[1]Thurber's older brother accidently shot him in the eye with an arrow when they were children, causing the immediate loss of that eye. He gradually lost the sight of the other eye because of complications from the accident and a cataract.

*Engell, J., & Dangerfield, A. (2007). *Saving higher education in the age of money*. Charlottesville, VA: University of Virginia Press.

4. Preparing List of References

Sample Entries: Articles in Print

When citing articles in print, provide the following categories of information. Whenever possible, copy the information directly from the print version of the article rather than the library catalogue or database. See the example on page 11.

1. **Author:** List all authors by last name, using only initials for first and middle names. Separate the names of multiple authors with commas, and use an ampersand (&) before the last author's name.

2. **Publication year:** Place the date of publication in parentheses immediately after the author's name, and place a period after the closing parenthesis.

3. **Title:** Cite the title of the article with sentence-style punctuation, without quotation marks, ending with a period.

4. **Journal:** Include the title of the journal with headline-style punctuation in italics followed by a comma.

5. **Volume/issue:** Place the volume number immediately after the comma in italics. Include the issue number—if any—in parentheses after the volume number, but do not use italics or a space between the volume and issue numbers.

6. **Pages:** Finish the citation by listing the inclusive pages (beginning and ending pages) of the article.

Arrange this information in the following pattern:

> Author. (Publication year). Title of the article. *Title of the Journal,*
>
> *Volume*(Issue), Inclusive pages.

For example, a citation for the article on page 11 would look like this:

1. An Article in a Journal

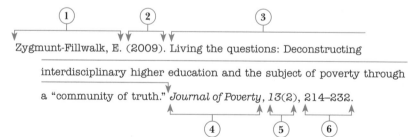

In-text citation: (Zygmunt-Fillwalk, 2009)

Entries illustrating variations on this basic format appear on pages 12–13.

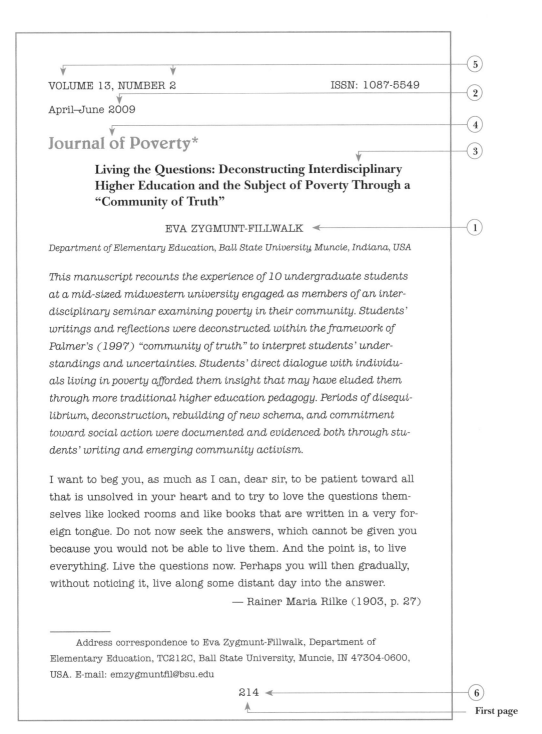

VOLUME 13, NUMBER 2 ⑤ ②

ISSN: 1087-5549

April–June 2009 ④

Journal of Poverty* ③

Living the Questions: Deconstructing Interdisciplinary Higher Education and the Subject of Poverty Through a "Community of Truth"

EVA ZYGMUNT-FILLWALK ← ①

Department of Elementary Education, Ball State University, Muncie, Indiana, USA

This manuscript recounts the experience of 10 undergraduate students at a mid-sized midwestern university engaged as members of an interdisciplinary seminar examining poverty in their community. Students' writings and reflections were deconstructed within the framework of Palmer's (1997) "community of truth" to interpret students' understandings and uncertainties. Students' direct dialogue with individuals living in poverty afforded them insight that may have eluded them through more traditional higher education pedagogy. Periods of disequilibrium, deconstruction, rebuilding of new schema, and commitment toward social action were documented and evidenced both through students' writing and emerging community activism.

I want to beg you, as much as I can, dear sir, to be patient toward all that is unsolved in your heart and to try to love the questions themselves like locked rooms and like books that are written in a very foreign tongue. Do not now seek the answers, which cannot be given you because you would not be able to live them. And the point is, to live everything. Live the questions now. Perhaps you will then gradually, without noticing it, live along some distant day into the answer.

— Rainer Maria Rilke (1903, p. 27)

Address correspondence to Eva Zygmunt-Fillwalk, Department of Elementary Education, TC212C, Ball State University, Muncie, IN 47304-0600, USA. E-mail: emzygmuntfil@bsu.edu

First page

2. An Article in a Journal with Continuous Paging

Farrell, A., & Givelber. (2010). Liberation reconsidered: Understanding why judges and juries disagree about guilt. *Journal of Criminal Law and Criminology, 100*, 1549–1586.

In-text citation: (Farrell & Givelber, 2010)

3. An Article with Separate Paging

Burruss, G. W., Wells, W., & Zeman, N. M. (2010). The ability of legitimate authorities to reduce academic misconduct. *Journal of Crime & Justice, 33*(2), 1–29.

In-text citation: (Burruss, Wells, & Zeman, 2010)

4. An Article in a Monthly Magazine

Freedman, D. H. (2011, February). How to fix the obesity crisis. *Scientific American, 304*(2), 40–47.

In-text citation: (Freedman, 2011)

5. An Article in a Newspaper

Grady, D. (2011, February 9). Lymph node study shakes breast cancer treatment. *New York Times*, pp. A1, A17.

In-text citation: (Grady, 2011)

6. An Abstract

Canary, H. E., & Canary, D. J. (2007). Making sense of one's career: An analysis and typology of supervisors' career studies. [Abstract]. *Communications Quarterly, 55*, 225–246.

In-text citation: (Canary & Canary, 2007)

7. A Letter to the Editor

Cox, E. (2010, November). [Letter to the editor] *Smithsonian, 41*(7), 8.

In-text citation: (Cox, 2010)

8. A Book Review

    Kolbert, E. (2011, January 31). [Review of *Battle hymn of the tiger mother*,

    by Amy Chua]. America's top parent. *The New Yorker*, 70–73.

    In-text citation: (Kolbert, 2011)

Sample Entries: Books in Print

When citing books in print, provide the following categories of information. Copy the information from the book's title page and copyright page (on the reverse side of the title page), not from the book's cover or from the library catalogue. See the example on page 14.

1. **Author:** List all authors by last name, and use only initials for the first and middle names. Separate the names with a comma, and use an ampersand (&) before the last author's name.

2. **Publication year:** Place the date of publication in parentheses immediately after the author's name. Place a period after the closing parenthesis.

3. **Title:** Italicize the title and subtitle, if any. Capitalize the first word of the book title and the first word of the subtitle.

4. **Place:** List place of publication. Include an abbreviation of the country or state if the city is unfamiliar. Separate the place and the publisher with a colon.

5. **Publisher:** Use the full name of the publisher, but omit words or abbreviations such as *Publisher, Company* and *Inc.*

Arrange this information in the following pattern:

> Author. (Publication year). *Title: Subtitle*. Place: Publisher.

For example, a citation for the book on page 14 would look like this:

1. A Book by One Author

Light, R. J. (2001). *Making the most of college: Students speak their minds.*

Cambridge, MA: Harvard University Press.

In-text citation: (Light, 2001)

Entries illustrating variations on this basic format appear on pages 15–17.

Title page

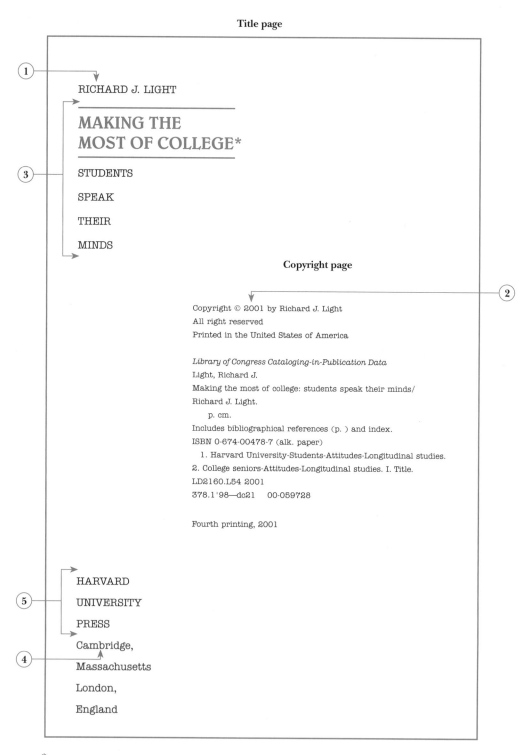

① RICHARD J. LIGHT

MAKING THE MOST OF COLLEGE*

③ STUDENTS

SPEAK

THEIR

MINDS

Copyright page

②

Copyright © 2001 by Richard J. Light
All right reserved
Printed in the United States of America

Library of Congress Cataloging-in-Publication Data
Light, Richard J.
Making the most of college: students speak their minds/
Richard J. Light.
    p. cm.
Includes bibliographical references (p.) and index.
ISBN 0-674-00478-7 (alk. paper)
   1. Harvard University-Students-Attitudes-Longitudinal studies.
2. College seniors-Attitudes-Longitudinal studies. I. Title.
LD2160.L54 2001
378.1'98—dc21   00-059728

Fourth printing, 2001

⑤ HARVARD

UNIVERSITY

PRESS

④ Cambridge,

Massachusetts

London,

England

*From Light, R. J. (2001). *Making the most of college: Students speak their minds.* Cambridge, MA: Harvard University Press.

2. Two or More Books by the Same Author—Arrange Chronologically

Florida, R. (2002). *The rise of the creative class . . . and how it's transforming work, leisure, community, & everyday life.* New York: Basic Books.

In-text citation: (Florida, 2002)

Florida, R. (2005). *The flight of the creative class: The new global competition for talent.* New York: HarperCollins.

In-text citation: (Florida, 2005)

Multiple Books by the Same Author in the Same Year—Arrange Alphabetically by Title

Sternberg, R. J. (Ed.). (2003a). *Psychologists defying the crowd: Stories of those who battled the establishment and won.* Washington, DC: American Psychological Association.

In-text citation: (Sternberg, 2003a)

Sternberg, R. J. (2003b). *Why smart people can be so stupid.* New Haven, CT: Yale University Press.

In-text citation: (Sternberg, 2003b)

3. A Book by Two or More Authors

Arum, R., & Roska, J. (2011). *Academically adrift: Limited learning on college campuses.* Chicago: University of Chicago Press.

In-text citation: (Arum & Roska, 2011)

4. A Book by an Anonymous Author

United Press International stylebook and guide to newswriting (4th ed.). (2004). Herndon, VA: Capital Books.

In-text citation: (*United Press International*, 2004)

5. A Book by a Group (e.g., organization, corporation)

American Psychological Association. (2009). *Publication manual of the American Psychological Association* (6th ed.). Washington, DC: Author.

In-text citation: (American Psychological Association [APA], 2009)

6. A Book with an Editor(s)

Wolfe, D. A., & Mash, E. J. (Eds.). (2005). *Behavioral and emotional disorders in adolescents: Nature assessment, and treatment.* New York:
Guilford Press.

In-text citation: (Wolfe & Mash, 2005)

7. An Edition After the First

Mehler, P. S., & Andersen, A. E. (2010). *Eating disorders: A guide to medical
care and complications* (2nd ed.). Baltimore, MD: Johns Hopkins
University Press.

In-text citation: (Mehler & Andersen, 2010)

8. A Translation

Steinberg, M. D. (2003). *Voices of revolution, 1919* (M. Schwartz, Trans.).
New Haven, CT: Yale University Press.

In-text citation: (Steinberg, 2003)

9. A Multivolume Work

Fisher, B. S., & Lab, S. P. (Eds.). (2010). *Encyclopedia of victimology and
crime prevention* (Vols. 1–2). Thousand Oaks, CA: Sage.

In-text citation: (Fisher & Lab, 2010)

10. A Chapter in an Edited Book

Jenkins, A. (2009). Supporting student development in and beyond the disciplines: The role of curriculum. In C. Kreber (Ed.), *The university and
its disciplines: Teaching and learning within and beyond disciplinary
boundaries* (pp. 157–168). New York: Routledge.

In-text citation: (Jenkins, 2009)

11. A Government Report

Executive Office of the President. (2003). *Economic report of the President,
2003* (GPO Publication No. 040-000-0760-1). Washington, DC: U.S.
Government Printing Office.

In-text citation: (Executive Office of the President, 2003)

12. A Selection from a Reference Book

Padgett, D. K. (1995). Homelessness. In A. E. D. Orto & R. P. Marinelli

(Eds.), *Encyclopedia of disability and rehabilitation* (pp. 372–378).

New York: Simon & Schuster Macmillan.

In-text citation: (Padgett, 1995)

13. A Book with a Title in Its Title

Marcus, L. (Ed.). (1999). *Sigmund Freud's* The interpretation of dreams:

New interdisciplinary essays. Manchester, England: University of

Manchester Press.

In-text citation: (Marcus, 1999)

Sample Entries: Online Publications

When citing online publications, follow the patterns for print sources (articles and books) when possible. But place information about how (and when) a source was retrieved at the end of the entry. See the example on page 19.

1. **Author:** List all authors by last name, using only initials for first and middle names. Separate the names of multiple authors with a comma, and use an ampersand (&) before the last author's last name.

2. **Publication year:** Place the date of publication in parentheses immediately after the author's name, and place a period after the closing parenthesis.

3. **Title:** Cite the title of an article with sentence-style punctuation, without quotation marks, ending with a period. Cite the title of a book with sentence-style punctuation in italics.

4. **Journal:** For articles, include the title of the journal in headline punctuation italics followed by a comma.

5. **Volume/issue:** For articles, place the volume number immediately after the comma italics. Include the issue number, if any, in parentheses after the volume number, but do not use italics or a space between the volume and issue numbers.

6. **Place:** For books, list the place of publication. Include an abbreviation of the country or state if the city is unfamiliar. Separate the place and publisher with a colon.

7. **Publisher:** For books, use the full name of the publisher, but omit words or abbreviations such as *Publisher, Company* and *Inc.*

8. **Pages:** For articles, finish the citation by listing the inclusive pages (beginning and ending pages) of the article.

9. **Retrieval information:** Current publications usually supply a DOI (digital object identifier) at the top of the first page of an article. When no DOI is available, use a URL (uniform resource locator). When retrieval information is likely to change, include the date when you accessed the information.

Arrange this information in the following pattern (article):

> Author. (Publication year). Title of the article. *Title of the Journal, Volume* (Issue), inclusive pages. Retrieval information, doi, or URL.

For example, a citation for the article on page 19 would look like this:

1. An Article from an Online Journal

Scullin, M. H., Kanaya, T., & Ceci, S. J. (2002). Measurement of individual differences in children's suggestibility across situation. *Journal of Experimental Psychology: Applied, 8*(4), 233–246.

doi: 10-1037/1076-898x.8.4.233

In-text citation: (Scullin, Kanaya, & Ceci, 2002)

Entries illustrating variations of this basic format appear on pages 20–21.

(8)

(9)

(4)

(5)

(2)

Journal of Experimental Psychology: Applied
2002, Vol. 8, No. 4, 233–246

Measurement of Individual Differences in Children's Suggestibility Across Situations*

(3)

(1)

Matthew H. Scullin, Tomoe Kanaya, and Stephen J. Ceci
Cornell University

The authors attempted to use scores on the Video Suggestibility Scale for Children (VSSC, M. H. Scullin & S. J. Ceci, 2001) to predict 50 preschool children's performance during a field study in which they were interviewed suggestively 4 times about both a true event and a suggested event. Among the 25 children over age 4 years 6 months, tendencies on the VSSC to respond affirmatively to suggestive questions ("yield"), change answers in response to negative feedback ("shift"), and the sum of these ("total suggestibility") were all related to lack of accuracy about the true event in the field study and to both accuracy and lack of accuracy about the suggested event. Results support a 2-factor model of suggestibility.

Since Alfred Binet's pioneering work on suggestiblity nearly 100 years ago (Cunningham, 1988), psychological researchers have conducted numerous studies to identify external or "situational" variables that affect children's testimony (see Ceci & Bruck, 1993, 1995, for reviews). More recently, researchers have begun to examine the characteristics within children that cause some to be more accurate than others (for reviews see Bruck, Ceci, & Melnyk, 1997; Quas, Qin, Schaaf, & Goodman, 1997). According to these reviews, there is a growing consensus that children's suggestibility entails an interplay between individual characteristics and situational factors and that further research is needed to examine this relationship in greater detail.

There are at least four reasons for examining the interplay between developmental, situational, and individual characteristics in detail: First, young children have been found to be more suggestible than adults or older children, with preschool children being the most suggestible (Ceci & Bruck, 1993).

Matthew H. Scullin, Tomoe Kanaya, and Stephen J. Ceci, Department of Human Development, Cornell University.

First page of article

2. An Article from a Database

Coyne, S. M., Robinson, S. L., & Nelson, D. A. (2010). Does reality back-
bite? Physical, verbal, and relational aggression in reality television.
Journal of Broadcasting & Electronic Media, 54(2), 282–298. Retrieved
from Academic Search Premier (50791713).

In-text citation: (Coyne, Robinson, & Nelson, 2010)

3. An Article in an Online Magazine

Jennings, K. (2011, February 16). My puny human brain. *Slate.* Retrieved
February 16, 2011, from http://www.slate.com/id/2284721/

In-text citation: (Jennings, 2011)

4. An Article from an Online Newspaper

Galland, L. (2011, February 17). Memory loss can be caused by over-
the-counter drugs. *The Huffington Post.* Retrieved February 17 from
http://huffintonpost.com/leo_galland_md/
memoryloss-drugs -_b_822245.html

In-text citation: (Galland, 2011)

5. An Online Book

Jackson, S. (2004). *Teaching children with deficit hyperactivity disorder: In-
structional strategies and practices.* Washington, DC: U.S. Department
of Education. Retrieved from http:// purl. Access.gpo.gov/
GPO/LPS49520

In-text citation: (Jackson, 2004)

6. An Article in an Online Encyclopedia or Other Reference Book

Campbell-Mohn, C. I., & Cheever, F. (2011). Environmental law. *Encyclopæ-
dia Britannica.* Retrieved from http://www.britannica.com/EBchecked/
topic/765435/environmental law

In-text citation: (Campbell-Mohn & Cheever, 2011)

7. An Authored Document from a Website

    Irons, S. (2010, March 1). Students seek family members of Alzheimer's pa-

    tients for educational video. Retrieved May 3, 2010, from http://www.

    bsu.edu/news/article/0,1370,7273-850-63777,00.html

    In-text citation: (Irons, 2010)

8. An Online Posting—Blog or Discussion Group

    Kellerman, M. (2007, May 23). Disclosing clinical trials. Message posted to

    http://www.iq.harvard.edu/blog/sss/archives/2007/05

9. An Entry in a Wiki

    Happiness. (2007, June 14). Retrieved March 30, 2008, from PsychWiki:

    http://www.psychwiki.com/wiki/Happiness

Sample Entries: Audiovisual and Miscellaneous Sources

Many of the sources listed in this section are rarely used in APA papers.
However, on occasion they can provide interesting support for your argument. Notice in the examples that brackets, [], are used to identify the
medium of the source.

1. A Motion Picture

    Hooper, T. (Director). (2010). *The king's speech.* [Motion picture]. [With C.

    Firth, G. Rush, & H. B. Carter]. United States: Momentum.

    In-text citation: (Hooper, 2010)

2. A Television Broadcast

    Kirk, M., & Smith, M. (Producers). (2011, February 22). Revolution in

    Cairo. [Television series episode]. In D. Fanning (Executive Producer),

    Frontline. Boston: WGBH.

    In-text citation: (Kirk & Smith, 2011)

3. A Radio Broadcast

    Gazit, C. (Producer). (2005, February 16). Seeds of destruction. [Radio

    series episode]. In D. J. James (Executive Producer), *Slavery and the

    making of America.* New York: WNET.

    In-text citation: (Gazit, 2005)

4. A Recording

Plant, R., & Krauss, A. (2007). Gone gone gone (done moved on). On T.

B. Burnett (Producer), *Raising sand* [CD]. Burlington, MA: Rounder

Records.

In-text citation: (Plant & Krauss, 2007)

5. A Work of Art

Hopper, E. (1930). *Early Sunday morning.* [Oil on canvas]. Whitney Museum

of Art. New York.

In-text citation: (Hopper, 1930)

6. A Lecture or Speech

Ramas, K. (2011, January 27). It ain't what you do, it's how you do it:

Global education for gender justice. Speech presented at the annual

meeting of the American Association of Colleges and Universities,

San Francisco, CA.

In-text citation: (Ramas, 2011)

5. APA Research Paper Format

See "Annotated Student Research Paper" (pages 25–31) for illustrations of each of the following features.

1. **Title page:** Although APA does not provide guidelines for the title page of an undergraduate research paper, a variation on the format suggested for professional researchers should meet the expectations of your instructor. As the first line on your title page, provide the words *Running head,* followed by a colon, 1 inch from the top of the page, flush left. (Note that "Running head," like other terms that come up later in this discussion, is *not* italicized on your actual paper; it appears that way here only due to the style parameters of this book.) After the colon provide a shortened version of your title—all in capital letters. Opposite the running head provide the page number 1, flush right. Center the complete title of your paper—double-space, if necessary— in headline-style capitalization. Provide double spacing between the next two items on the page: your name, and then the name of your

school. Some instructors may ask you to include additional lines to identify their name and the name of the course.

2. **Abstract:** The abstract is the second page of your paper. Three lines below the running head, type and center the word *Abstract.* Two lines below this word begin a paragraph that provides a summary of your thesis and the main issues you address in your paper. This paragraph—double-spaced and not indented—should be 250 words or less. You may want to include a list of keywords two lines below your abstract. Type *Keywords*—and this time in actual italics—followed by a colon, and a list of a few words that you think are "key" to the argument in your paper.

3. **Text:** The text proper, double-spaced throughout, begins on page 3. The running head—all in capital letters—appears flush left on every page of your paper. Three lines below the running head, center your complete title in headline-style capitalization. Two lines below the title begin your paper using indented paragraphs and double spacing between paragraphs. Follow the pattern indicated for quotations, summaries, paraphrases, and in-text citation discussed on pages 4–6.

4. **Headings:** Although headings are not required, APA encourages their use—especially in longer papers—to help readers follow the organization of your paper. These headings are centered in boldface and announce a new section of your paper.

5. **References:** Your list of references appears as a separate and numbered page after the last page of your text. Continue to use your running head, flush left, and the page number, flush right. Center the title, "References," 1 inch below the running head. List your references in alphabetical order, following the patterns suggested in "Preparing List of References," pages 10–22. Type the first line flush left, and then indent any subsequent lines 0.5 inch (or five spaces). Double-space after (impossible to space "between" a single line) each line and between each entry.

6. **Notes:** If you decide to create a notes page, as opposed to placing individual footnotes at the bottom of the appropriate page, then this page appears as a separate and numbered page after your list of references. Follow the same pattern you have used throughout by including your running head, flush left, and a page number, flush right. Then 1 inch below your running head, type and center the word *Notes* (but, again, not actually in italics). Your notes should appear in numerical order, following the same sequence in which they appear in the text. Each note is double-spaced in paragraph style, with the first line following the number indented and subsequent lines aligned at the left margin. Double-space after each note.

6. Annotated Student Research Paper

(A dog, sitting at a computer terminal, talking to another dog.) Published in *The New Yorker* 7/5/1993 by Peter Steiner SKU:106197

"On the Internet, nobody knows you're a dog."

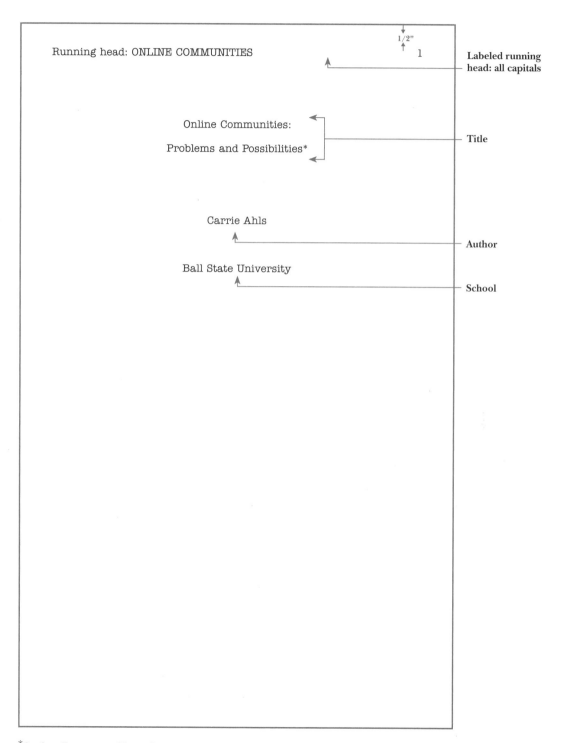

Running head: ONLINE COMMUNITIES   1/2"   1

Labeled running head: all capitals

Online Communities:

Problems and Possibilities*

Title

Carrie Ahls

Author

Ball State University

School

*Student Essay created by author

Centered label with normal capitalization

Keywords

1/2"

Abstract

In recent years, researchers have tried to access the impact of online communities on the people who join them and the people who are affected by them. There is certainly evidence to suggest that participation in such communities may have many unintended negative consequences. But there is also increasing evidence that participating in such communities will have a transformative effect on virtual and real communities. This paper discusses the research about both the problems and possibilities of online communities and points to the role individual responsibility has in determining how such communities will function.

Keywords: cyber abuse, Internet addiction, citizen-based democracy

Text begin on page 3

Online Communities:

Problems and Possibilities

Centered title with headline-style capitalization

The emergence of online social networks has raised controversial questions about the meaning of identity and community in cyberspace. For example, to what extent do the identities participants craft for online communication match their real identity? And to what extent does a virtual community approximate the traditions and values associated with real face-to-face communities? These questions have prompted many researchers to point to the abuses of online communication. However, other researchers, while acknowledging the potential dangers of online communication, remain enthusiastic about the educational value of social networks and their importance to democracy and citizenship.

A major abuse often encountered in the virtual world is "cyberbullying." According to McKenna (2007), "cyberbullying" is "sending threatening messages, displaying private messages, and posting embarrassing video photos online" (p. 26). McKenna explained that by assuming a false identity, a person could enter the supposedly safe world of a chat room and spread all sorts of destructive information about other members of the online community. Because the targets of such bullying have no way to correct the destructive information, they can become extremely depressed. Malone (2007) reported that a 13-year-old girl from suburban St. Louis committed suicide after being continually taunted in her MySpace profile (p. 13).

A related abuse is "cyberstalking." According to a report from the United States Department of Justice, *1999 Report on Cyberstalking:*

Past tense to report scholarship

Specific reference: author, date, and page

Page number enclosed within parenthesis

General reference: government document

A New Challenge for Law Enforcement and Industry, online stalking is similar to real-world stalking. Both stalkers engage in repeated and unwelcome threatening sexual behavior. However, online stalkers can explore online communities, such as dating sites, to gain extensive personal information about their victims. The report acknowledged that while online stalking may not involve physical contact, it may serve as a "prelude to more serious behavior, including physical violence" (U.S. Department of Justice, 1999). Zeller reported a particularly sinister case of cyberstalking: the stalker not only bombarded his victim, an innocent 44-year-old publishing executive in Manhattan, with menacing sexual threats, but he also encouraged others to stalk her by posting her "full name address and phone number, along with a solicitation to call and drop by her home" (Zeller, 2006).

The cause of these online abuses and many other problems associated with online social networks is "Internet addiction." Like other forms of addiction—drug abuse, alcoholism, and gambling—Internet addiction is a compulsive behavior caused by the need to escape everyday problems. Young (1998) pointed out some of the signs of Internet addiction:

Long quotation: passages 40 words or more

> If we feel isolated, we can pour out our repressed feelings and act out hidden aspects of ourselves in meeting rooms and interactive games. If we long for love and affection, but fear rejection or AIDS, we can cruise for cybersex. And if we are bored with our family or cynical about society, we can retreat into a subculture of Internet addicts who offer support, encouragement, excitement and

ONLINE COMMUNITIES   5

        intrigue, and maybe even an invitation to come run away

        from it all. (pp. 29–30)*

Working with the strategies used to diagnose other compulsive

disorders, Young devised a questionnaire that asked Internet users

questions such as "Do you feel restless, moody, depressed or irritable

when attempting to cut down on Internet use?" (p. 3). Respondents to

the questionnaire who Young classified as addicts admitted that they

"were investing more and more time online at a greater and greater

cost to their real lives" (p. 5).

    Although the accessibility of online communication provides

opportunities for abuse and addiction, many researchers remain

convinced that online social networks extend and enrich the way

participants experience the world. In particular, individuals who are

trapped or excluded by disabilities express feelings of liberation as a

result of their ability to communicate online. Cooper (2007) reported

such a case in *Alter Egos: Avatars and Their Creators.* Jason Rowe, a se-

verely handicapped boy from Crosby, Texas, explained how the virtual

world changed his sense of identities and community:

        Online it doesn't matter what you look like. . . . In the real

        world, people can be uncomfortable around me before they

        get to know me and realize that, apart from my outer ap-

        pearance, I'm just like them. . . . The internet eliminates

        how you look in real life, so you get to know a person by

        their mind and personality. (n.p.)**

In addition to liberation, researchers have reported that users of

social networks feel enriched by their ability to communicate with and

*Young, K. (1998). *Caught in the net: How to recognize the signs of internet addiction—and a winning strategy for recovery.* New York: Wiley.

**Cooper, R. (2007). *Alter egos: Avatars and their creators.* London: Chais Boot.

Documentation: the parenthetical references to long quotation follows the final mark of punctuation

Long quotation: quote from book with no page numbers

understand people all over the world. Diehl and Prins (2008) reported
that "participation in 'SL' [Second Life] enhanced Residents' intercultural literacy" (p. 102). Their research also revealed that "SL" participants gained a "greater awareness of insider cultural perspectives
and openness toward new viewpoints" (p. 102).

Short quotation: quote worked into writer's own sentence

Many researchers have argued that the most promising pros-
pects for online social networks is their ability to "revitalize citizen
based democracy" (Rheingold, 1999, xxix). The most compelling
example of how such networks can reconnect alienated citizens to
the political process is the recent revolution in Egypt. Regan (2011)
reported that the revolution was organized and driven by the "pro-
liferation of cheap technology and social media" (n.p.). The young
protesters in Cairo were able to by-pass the state controlled media,
communicate with one another without fear of being arrested, and
report on their victories to people across the world.

Summary of major issues in reference

Such events suggest that the possibilities and problems in the
virtual world may be no different than the possibilities and problems
in the real world. Both worlds enable you to find ideas, share information, connect with other people, and contribute to your community.
Both worlds also allow you to disguise your identity, abuse other
people and escape into fantasies. How you participate in both worlds
is up to you. Dyson (1997) argued that what you do online could or
should change your offline life "by making you less willing to accept
things the way they are and more sure of your ability to build a life
to suit yourself and your family" (p. 280).

Documentations author's name used to introduce quote

ONLINE COMMUNITIES   7

Sequential page numbers

References

Description title centered

Cooper, R. (2007). *Alter egos: Avatars and their creators.* London: Chais
Boot.

Diehl, W. C., & Prins, E. (2008). Unintended outcomes in "SL": Intercultural literacy and cultural identity in a virtual world. *Language and Intercultural Communication, 8*(2), 101–118.

Dyson, E. (1997). *Release 2.0: A design for living in the digital age.* New
York: Broadway.

Malone, R. (2007). Online harassment—a hoax, a suicide—a journalis-
tic dilemma. *St. Louis Journalism Review, 37*(301), 13. Retrieved
from http://issuu.com/sjreview/doc/december_2007_entire

McKenna, P. (2007). The rise of cyberbullying. *New Scientist, 195,*
26–27. Retrieved from Academic Search Premier (02624079).

Regan, B. (2011, February 13). Local man studying in Cairo wit-
nesses, recounts revolution. *The City Paper.* Retrieved from
http://nashvillecitypaper.com/content/city-news/local
man-studying-cairo-witn

Rheingold, H. (2000). *The virtual community: Homesteading on the
electronic frontier.* Cambridge, MA: MIT University Press.

United States Department of Justice, Attorney General. (1999). *1999
Report on cyberstalking: A new challenge for law enforcement and
industry.* Washington, DC: Author. Retrieved from http://purl._
Access.gpo.gov/GPO/LPS230367

Young, K. (1998). *Caught in the net: How to recognize the signs of Internet
addiction—and a winning strategy for recovery.* New York: Wiley.

Zeller, T., Jr. (2006, April 17). A sinister web entraps victims of
cyberstalking. *New York Times.* Retrieved from http://nytimes.
com/2006/4/17/technology/17stalk.html

Double-space

Sample entry: article in print

Indent five spaces

Sample entry: retrieval statement

Sample entry: book

Sample entry: government publications

Sample entry: newspaper

Index